DROITWICH
IN OLD PHOTOGRAPHS

SAL SAPIT OMNIA

DROITWICH.

REGD
TRADE MARK.

HERALDIC SERIES.

SALT FLAVOURS EVERYTHING

DROITWICH
IN OLD PHOTOGRAPHS

FROM THE COLLECTION OF
J.O. BRETTELL

ALAN SUTTON
1987

Alan Sutton Publishing Limited
Brunswick Road . Gloucester

First published 1987

British Library Cataloguing in Publication Data

Droitwich in old photographs.
1. Droitwich (Hereford and Worcester)—History
I. Brettell, J.O.
942.4'49   DA690.D7/

ISBN 0–86299–421–7

Typesetting and origination by
Alan Sutton Publishing Limited
Printed in Great Britain
by Redwood Burn Limited.

CONTENTS

INTRODUCTION

DROITWICH SPA

Now that we have the Brine Baths back in operation, I prefer to use the word 'Spa', where appropriate, after our town name, to tell the world that we are back in business as a 'Spa' Centre. It is a modest town, which over the last two decades, has had to suffer the scars of modernisation, together with reaping the benefits (?) of this so called progress.

Some very fine books have been written about the town, its people and its history, but to my knowledge, there has not been one devoted to pictures. Hence this humble offering, which I hope, will fill that gap. All you see in the following pages are from my own collection, and written up from personal knowledge derived from local people, the library and record archives. Of course nobody is perfect, and I am sure that I have made some mistakes with dates, people and places. However I do not think that they will change the course of the world, and that you will forgive this lapse from perfection. I would be delighted to hear from anyone with constructive criticism and corrections to any of the texts that I have used.

The photographs in this book are mainly of the buildings and roads of Droitwich, as it used to be, up to nearly one hundred years ago. This is aimed at the newer residents of our lovely town, who probably have no idea what Droitwich used to look like, before the development over the last few decades.

The ground on which Droitwich stands is rich in minerals and history, and it has progressed quite independently from the world of fashion, and everything from the time of the Romans, even up until now, has revolved around the magic word of *salt*.

If you were to ask anyone in Droitwich 'what name do you associate with salt?', the answer of course would be John Corbett. So much has been written about him that I would never try to compete with those words of learning. However, as a brief picture of this wonderful man, he was born in 1817 to Hannah and Joseph Corbett, who operated barges around the Black Country canals. Some sort of education followed, and when he was eleven he went to work for his father, and it was from him that he learnt the very basics of engineering. In his early twenties he was apprenticed to an engineering company, to eventually join his father on the narrow boats, until, with the coming of the train, they could see that there was not a big future on the canals, so they grasped the opportunity to sell out. Father retired, and John, with his share of the sale, bought the land from the liquidators of the British Alkali Co. at Stoke Works. This is where the connection with salt started, and after many years' of hard work, buying more land, leases and salt works, John Corbett was on his way to being the Salt King. Streets, houses, hotels, stations, hospitals and so many other assets to Droitwich are all due to his generosity and goodwill – as you turn the pages of this little book these will be very apparent.

Since those times, Droitwich has faltered and then prospered, until now in 1987–88 it is a busy industrial area, developing in it's own right, together with the new Brine Baths, to complete a full circle. The population has increased many times, and the old parts of Droitwich which have escaped the developer's eye are surrounded by new estates and factories – for the benefit of all concerned?

If you make this little book the success that I hope it will be, then I hope that next year I shall be able to publish another 'picture book'. This will be based on further Droitwich photographs and the surrounding villages – with more of an accent on people than in this book. This is where I want the help from the people of Droitwich Spa, to lend me their precious photographs, postcards and pictures, so that they may be copied and used in this next book, with the usual credits of course, for everybody's enjoyment.

I hope that you obtain as much pleasure from reading and looking at this book, as my wife and I have when we compiled it.

SECTION ONE
Views

DROITWICH

ST. RICHARDS MEMORIAL AND DODDERIL CHURCH

VICTORIA SQUARE

OLD COCK INN

NORBURY HOTEL

ST. ANDREWS BRINE BATHS

ROYAL BRINE BATHS

ON HOLIDAY, OR JUST TO SAY 'I AM GETTING BETTER', the best way was to show your friends where you were staying. Here are some views of the town over the next few pages, which highlight the places of interest.

SECTION TWO

Salt

Brine Pump, Droitwich

63408

WHERE IT ALL BEGAN — the machine that pumped the brine to the surface, at Covercroft, Droitwich.

THE BIG WHEEL OF A PUMPING ENGINE at Covercroft about 1900, operated by Mr William Evans at the Mitre Pit.

TWO FINE LOOKING LADY SALT WORKERS, who, for twelve hours a day, stirred and watched the simmering salt pans – all for ten bob a week!

THE MASSIVE EVAPORATING VATS above the ever hungry fires.

ANOTHER VIEW OF THE EVAPORATING VATS.

ONE OF THE ARTIFICIAL LAKES OF SALT at Covercroft. Whilst one worker agitates the briny mixture with a rake, others shovel salt into barrows.

BULK SALT being packed into sacks that must weigh about two and a half hundredweight.

This picture, taken about ninety years ago, shows the steaming salt pan, with Adam Crowther cutting a square of salt into shape, while behind, William Colley, Joe Farr and James Bourne manhandle the salt tubs extracted from the steaming mass.

Seems to be the same four men, plus one other, stacking away the salt cubes.

IN THIS DRYING HOUSE, KNOWN AS A STOVE, at Covercroft, blocks of salt were stacked in tunnel formation to allow the circulation of air, before being placed on the hot 'flue' running along the wall on the right.

SALT WORKERS 'pose' for their picture loading salt.

JOE FARR AND JAMES BOURNE preparing the salt tubs prior to filling.

SALT CUBES being put together for storage.

A DELIVERY OF BRINE CRYSTALS to London, for onward distribution.

A POSTCARD that advertises salt on the one side, and has the address and message on the other.

SECTION THREE

The Hospitals

t. John's Brine Baths Hospital, Droitwich Spa

THE HOSPITAL situated in St Peter's Walk, is a fine structure of red brick with terracotta facings, and was built in 1892 by a Mrs. T.W. Williams at a cost of about £5000 — so it says in the 1921 issue of Kelly's Directories! Also, if you subscribed three guineas a year, you were entitled to send one patient to the hospital — baths, board and lodging and medical advice being provided on payment of ten shillings per week.

MEN'S DINING ROOM.

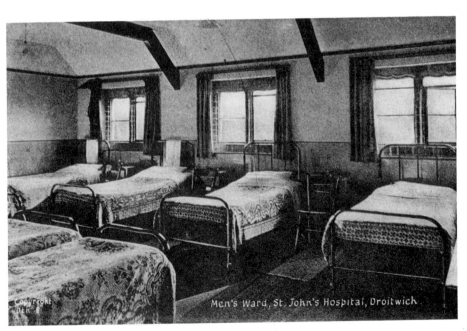

THE MEN'S WARD.

WOMEN'S DINING ROOM.

PATIENTS RELAXING in the sun outside the hospital.

WOMEN'S SITTING ROOM.

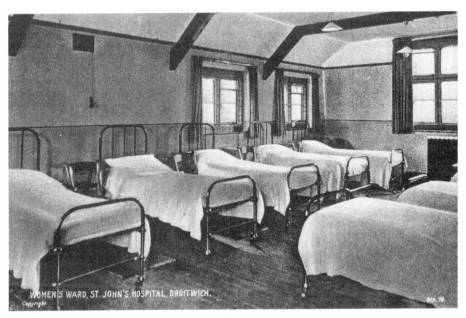

WOMEN'S WARD.

THE BIRMINGHAM HOSPITAL SATURDAY AND SUNDAY FUND purchased this property, and after vast alterations and additions it became the Highfield Hospital. Most of the patients at this time came from the Birmingham area to receive the benefits of the Droitwich brine.

THE LOUNGE

MEN'S SITTING ROOM.

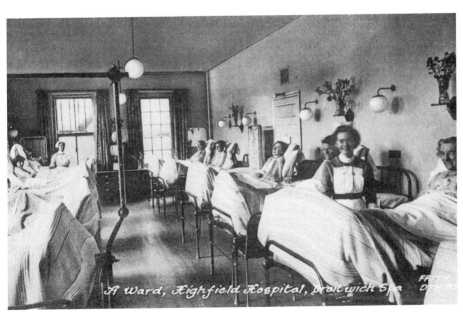

A WARD AT THE HOSPITAL.

THE OAKLANDS was at one time the home of the Bradley family, shown here as a Convalescent Home, it was then a Children's Home, and is now demolished in favour of a housing estate.

THE DINING ROOM AT THE OAKLANDS.

SECTION FOUR

Comic Cards

Blue Bells
from
DROITWICH

IN THE LATE VICTORIAN AND EARLY EDWARDIAN YEARS, comic and slightly *risqué* cards were all the rage. The best known artist, Cynicus, produced some very funny cards – some are shown on the following pages.

We are having a grand time at Droitwich

Considering everything, we are fairly comfortable at Droitwich

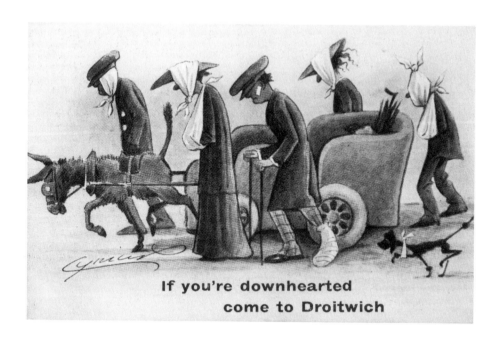

Hotel Life in
Droitwich

In the Briny
at Droitwich

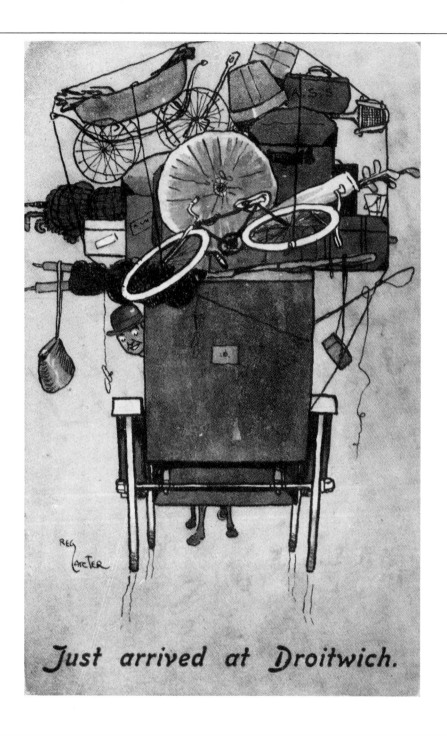

Just arrived at Droitwich.

Churches

THE CHURCH OF THE SACRED HEART AND SAINT CATHERINE OF ALEXANDRIA was built after the pattern of a Roman Basilica, and displays an outstanding example of Byzantine-style mosaic work. This is a view of the church from the main road.

LITANY OF THE SAINTS

THE LAYING OF THE FOUNDATION STONE of the church by The Most Reverend John McIntyre, Auxiliary Bishop of Birmingham, on the Feast of Saint Catherine of Alexandria on 25 November 1919. In the course of the laying of the stone, the Bishop and the congregation knelt and recited the Litany of The Saints. In 1921 the church was blessed and opened by the same Reverend John McIntyre, who, in the mean time, had become the Archbishop of Birmingham.

THE INTERIOR OF THE CHURCH showing the beautiful mosaic.

THE APSE.

SAINT CATHERINE OF ALEXANDRIA.

ST RICHARD blesses the Droitwich Salt Springs.

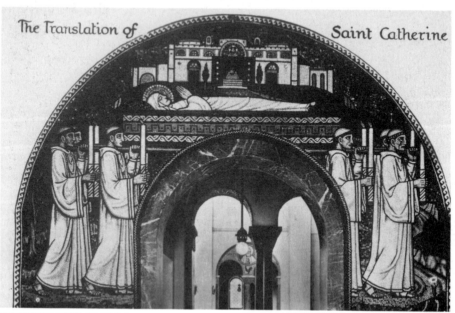

THE TRANSLATION OF ST CATHERINE.

ST FRANCIS preaching to the birds.

SAINT RICHARD IS BAPTIZED AT DROITWICH

SAINT RICHARD is baptised at Droitwich.

THE CORONATION OF THE BLESSED VIRGIN.

ST CATHERINE disputes with the doctors, and the Martyrdom of the doctors.

St. Andrews Church, Droitwich.

ST ANDREW'S CHURCH.

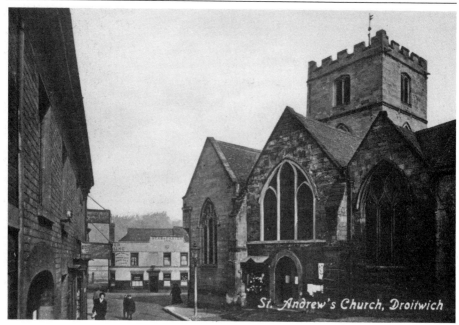

THE CHURCH – looking down St Andrews Street.

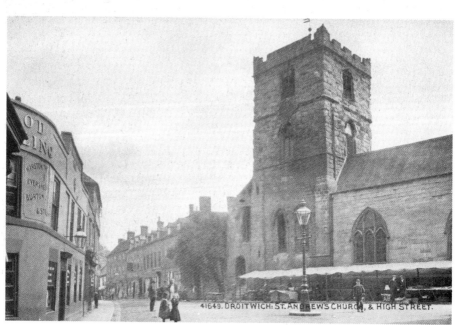

THE MARKET STALLS in the lee of the church.

ST NICHOLAS CHURCH, DROITWICH.

THE INTERIOR OF THE CHURCH.

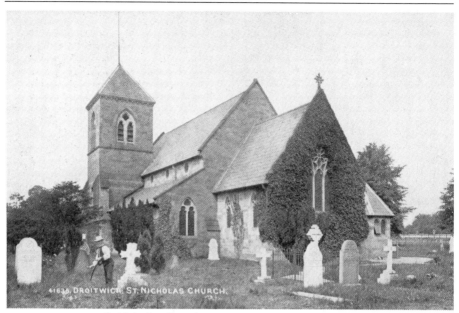

THE GARDENER (?) at St Nicholas Church.

THE BAPTIST CHURCH, Ombersley Street.

THREE LITTLE IMPS (!) at the Lychgate.

S 13342 St. Peter's Church, Droitwich

THE LYCHGATE at St Peter's.

TWO FINE SHOTS OF THE INTERIOR OF THE CHURCH.

THE HARVEST nearly safely gathered in.

A VIEW OF THE CHURCH across the graveyard.

WYLDE'S MONUMENT ST PETER'S DROITWICH.

IN THE NORTH TRANSEPT is an imposing monument to George Wylde resting uncomfortably on his elbow. He was Lord Chief Baron of the exchequer under Thomas Cromwell.

ST AUGUSTINE'S CHURCH, Dodderhill.

ST RICHARD'S MEMORIAL and the church.

THE INTERIOR of St Augustine's Church.

A GENERAL VIEW OF THE CHURCH.

OVER THE VINES to the church.

A BARGE on the canal below the church.

THE CHURCH FROM ANOTHER ANGLE.

Hotels and Guest Houses

Raven Hotel, Droitwich.

THE RAVEN HOTEL. The original building on this site dates back many years, and in its lifetime has changed hands very infrequently. It has been burnt to the ground, rebuilt, altered and then in 1879 bought by John Corbett, further developed and eventually opened as The Raven Hotel in 1887. It was later purchased by the Platts family, and, via father and son, was run to a high standard, and then recently sold again.

THE TENNIS COURT.

THE UPPER LAWN.

THE GROUND FLOOR BEDROOMS.

THE PUTTING GREEN.

THE DINING ROOM.

THE SUN LOUNGE.

S.19760. SUN RAYS. DROITWICH.

THE SUNRAYS HOTEL. Another of the smaller hotels catering for the patients who came to Droitwich for medical help. Now a home for the elderly and retired.

ST ANDREW'S HOUSE HOTEL. A small privately run hotel, that offers right up to today, the best in food, wine and service.

A further two pictures of the St Andrew's hotel and gardens.

AYRSHIRE HOUSE HOTEL. Another of the hotels that were in Droitwich to accomodate patients for the Brine Baths. However in its later life it became, for a few years, an office block, and now is a home for those who need care and attention.

THE DINING ROOM

THE PARK HOTEL. Another of John Corbett's interests – now The Heriots Old People's Home.

THE VIEW FROM THE ENTRANCE HALL.

THE WORCESTERSHIRE BRINE BATHS HOTEL. The Worcestershire Hotel came into being when a local builder went bankrupt, and John Corbett purchased two unfinished houses from him. He then completed the buildings as a hotel, and subsequent owners have extended and modernised it to become what we see today. The hotel was opened in 1891 by the Countess of Dudley of Witley Court.

MENU

OPENING DINNER,   NOV. 4TH, 1891.

OF THE

Worcestershire Brine Baths Hotel, Droitwich,

GIVEN BY

JOHN CORBETT, ESQ.

Soups.

PRINTANIERE   OX-TAIL.

Fish.

FILLETS OF SOLES IN ASPIC.

Entrée.

JUGGED HARE WITH JELLY.

Cold Dishes.

ROAST BEEF.   SMOKED YORK HAM.

CHICKEN BECHAMEL.

LAMB AND MINT SAUCE.   PRESSED BEEF

ROAST CHICKEN.   ROAST TURKEY.

Sweets.

APPLE TARTS.   COMPOTE OF FRUITS

FRENCH PASTRY.   MERINGUES À LA CRÈME.

STEWED PEARS.   BAKED CUSTARD.

CHEESE AND CELERY.

DESSERT.

R. P. CULLEY, Proprietor.

AN ORIGINAL MENU used at the opening of the hotel, 4 November 1891

THE MAIN DRIVE, entrance to the hotel.

LOOKING EAST along the front of the hotel.

THE GARDENS of the hotel.

THE VERY ORNATE DRAWING ROOM.

A MEET OF THE WORCESTERSHIRE HOUNDS at the hotel – it still happens today.

A MORNING BAND PERFORMANCE in the gardens of the hotel.

THE GREAT WESTERN HOTEL, adjacent to the station, since demolished and now the site for the Girl Guide Headquarters.

RICHMOND HOUSE, A well known boarding house in Ombersley Street.

IMPNEY – THE CREATION OF JOHN CORBETT. It was no mean house that John Corbett, the famous salt manufacturer and philanthropist, built for his bride in the years 1870–1875. It took the place of the Manor House, set in acres of Dodderhill Parish, and a splendid mansion rose above the trees of the beautiful Worcestershire countryside, modelled on a sixteenth century French château. He called it Impney and to many people it has been a landmark for all to see and marvel at. After Corbett's death, it led rather a chequered life, from private house to hotel, requisitioned during the last war, and then bought by Ralph Edwards. He, with his foresight, could see that it could be developed into a beautiful hotel and become the Mecca for all those who liked the good life – and this he did. It was Mr Edwards that added the word 'Château' to its name, and there are not many people in the Midlands who have not heard of The Château Impney.

THE RECEPTION HALL.

THE RIVER SALWARPE at Impney.

THE BALLROOM.

THE WINTER GARDENS RESTAURANT.

THE BEAUTIFUL GARDENS.

IMPNEY LODGE AND GATES.

ABBEY CROFT GUEST HOUSE. Union Lane. Now demolished.

WESTCROFT VILLA GUEST HOUSE. Ombersley Street.

RODENGRANT GUEST HOUSE, Worcester Road.

THE ELMS GUEST HOUSE, Ombersley Street.

Randolph Private Hotel, Droitwich

THE RANDOLPH PRIVATE HOTEL, Now a hairdresser and restaurant.

CLARENDON HOUSE — halfway up, (or is it down?), St Andrew's Street.

Streets, Roads and Avenues

Old Cock Inn, Droitwich

THE OLD COCK INN is steeped in history, having gained its first licence in 1712, during the reign of Queen Anne. It has a curious frontage, having a window from the old St Nicholas Church, and also a stone replica of the head of the infamous Judge Jefferies.

THE NORBURY HOUSE HOTEL before further alterations made it give way to conversion into flats and the well-known and delightful theatre.

A LOVELY VIEW of Friar Street looking west.

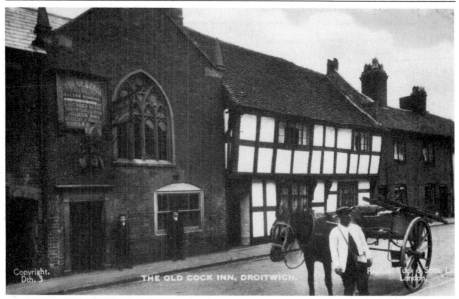

DELIVERIES BY HORSE AND CART were the norm in these days.

PRIORY HOUSE is an Elizabethan house which was restored to its present glory a few years ago.

A FAMILY AFTERNOON WALK down a very quiet street!

Most photographs of Friar Street always seem to highlight the Old Cock weather vane above the roof.

Corbett Avenue,
Droitwich Spa

THE HALF-FINISHED HYDRO HOTEL, through the trees on the right.

ST MARGARET'S, Corbett Avenue.

A PONY-DRAWN BATH CHAIR, used to collect the patients about 1929.

OAKLEY STREET, before it became an extension of Corbett Avenue.

The Holloway, Droitwich. 60604

A LEAFY LANE, which is now a busy main town artery from Hanbury Road to Tagwell Road.

WORCESTER ROAD AT WITTON.

THE ENTRANCE TO THE BRINE BATHS PARK from Worcester Road.

A QUIET DRIVE along Worcester Road.

WITTON – note the horse-drawn Landeau.

LOOKING UP WITTON HILL.

LOOKING DOWN WITTON HILL

Where Worcester Road and Queen Street meet the High Street.

CHAPEL BRIDGE and Queen Street.

QUEEN STREET looking towards Chapel Bridge.

THE OLD COACH ROAD, WITTON.

AGRICULTURAL SHOW. 4–6 June 1912.

A 'BUSY' HIGH STREET SCENE.

EXPRESS DELIVERY by horse and cart early this century.

HIGH STREET looking west.

HIGH STREET and The Waggon and Horses, or Crooked House as it was known locally.

THE MYSTERIOUS TABLE IN THE SMOKE ROOM of the Crooked House, which to all appearances is slanting at an angle of 30° – but a billiard ball placed on what looks like the lower end, disregards the law of gravity and cheerfully rolls uphill.

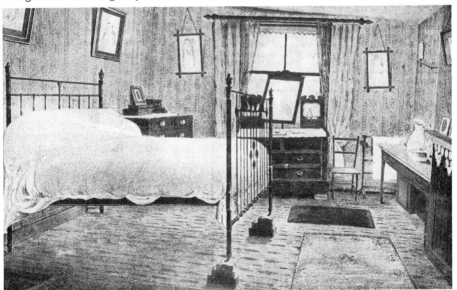

HERE THE BEDS ARE TIED TO THE WALL, and the castors are taken off one end and packed up to nine inches at the other to make it level!

This part of Droitwich, being at the lowest level, suffered from floods many times – this one, as the one overleaf, in June 1924.

HIGH STREET FLOOD – June 1924.

HIGH STREET, LOOKING UP — to me, that should be looking down.

THE 'TOP' OF THE HIGH STREET, showing to the left that lovely old black and white building, for many years the home of Harris the Chemist.

THE JUNCTION OF THE HIGH STREET AND ST ANDREWS STREET.

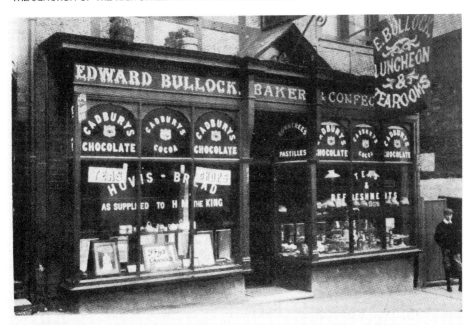

E. BULLOCK, Fancy White and Brown Bread Baker, Pastry=Cook and Confectioner,
HIGH STREET, DROITWICH.

AN ADVERTISEMENT CARD FOR BULLOCK'S CAFE.

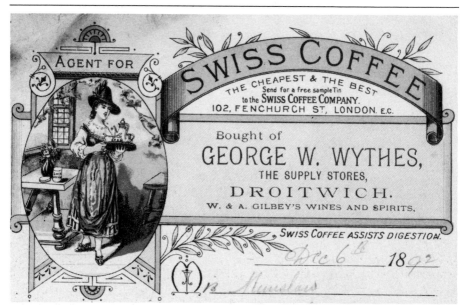

AN ACCOUNT FROM GEORGE W. WYTHES, the well-known High Street grocer. 6 December 1892.

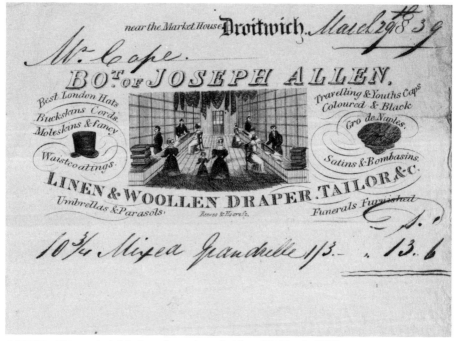

ANOTHER ACCOUNT, but this time from Joseph Allen. 29 March 1839.

Not a good thing to try in Station Street today!

A novel way to announce your arrival time.

LOOKING ALONG OMBERSLEY STREET, from the Raven Hotel.

THE LOWER END OF OMBERSLEY STREET, towards the station.

Salters Hall and Victoria Square

Droitwich, Salters Hall.

WORK ON BUILDING THE OLD SALTERS HALL began in 1879, and was eventually opened with much pomp and ceremony in 1881, before a large and distinguished audience. Now the people of Droitwich at last had a hall, capable of holding up to 1500 people, which could be used for meetings, lectures and anything else that could be thought up for such a wonderful building. However, times change, and in 1933 the old Hall was demolished, and there rose from the rubble, a year or so later, a fine looking cinema, with a cafe and shops below. Cinemas lost their appeal, and after standing empty for some little time, has, as we all know today, been reborn as a library.

A LOVELY VIEW OF SALTERS HALL with the horse-drawn bath chairs waiting for customers.

LOOKING TOWARDS ST ANDREWS STREET between the Salters Hall and the Raven Hotel.

ANOTHER QUIET DAY IN THE SQUARE, c. 1910.

LOOKING TOWARDS THE RAVEN HOTEL and the old Salters Hall.

TWO SHOTS OF THE SALTERS HALL c. 1930.

YOUNG LADIES IN SCHOOL UNIFORM(?) pass the Salters Hall.

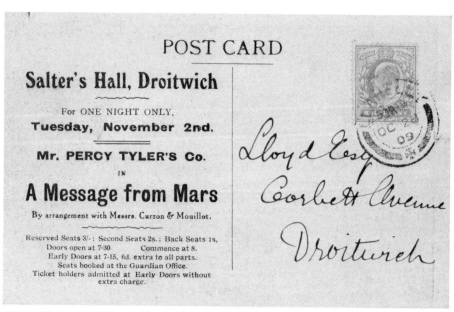

IF YOU WERE SOMEBODY — you had a direct invitation!

41646. DROITWICH: VICTORIA SQUARE.

PLENTY OF PARKING SPACE here in the Square c. 1900.

Droitwich Spa, Victoria Square.

FRITH.
DTH·49.

VICTORIA SQUARE looking towards Ombersley Street.

MIDLAND RED BUS STOP opposite the Raven Garage.

A REAR VIEW OF THE NEW SALTERS HALL, with the spire of the Worcestershire Hotel in the middle right.

THE GPO AND BANK in Ombersley Street.

VICTORIA SQUARE.

VICTORIA SQUARE, DROITWICH.

THE NATIONAL PROVINCIAL BANK and the new Post Office in the distance.

ANOTHER VIEW OF THE POST OFFICE, without a queue?

People, Personalities and other Interesting Pictures.

A FINE PICTURE OF JAMES HARRIS AND HIS SON.

COVENTRY CHARITY ALMSHOUSES. Dozens of elderly people in Droitwich have benefited from a huge wager made on the horses, more than three hundred years ago! At a dinner party given by the then Lord Sandys at his home, Ombersley Court, in the mid 1600s, two aristocrats became involved in a costly gamble, which was to have a lasting impact. Sir Henry Coventry of Croome Court, and Sir John Pakington of Westwood Park, each boasted that they owned the fastest racehorse in the country. The only way to resolve this was to have a race, and this encounter took place at Westwood Park. The enormous wager on the outcome was that the loser should build a welfare institution for the needy Droitwich folk, and name it after the winner. The race was won by Sir Henry Coventry's horse, but it is said that the loser could not pay up in cash at the time. Instead Sir John transferred two of his farms on the Westwood Estate to the victor. Sir Henry then honoured the wager on his death, when he bequeathed £1000 in his will to buy a piece of land in Droitwich, and build the welfare institution.

Coventry Charity Almhouses, Droitwich

Valentines Series

38699

THREE OF THE OLDEST FEMALE INHABITANTS at the Almshouses. c.1905.

A SUPERB DISPLAY OF MEAT by Mr Kendrick, the butcher, at the corner of North Street and Ombersley Street.

No doubt there would be howls of dismay from any Traffic Inspector at the sight of Everton's steam lorry and trailer, so very heavily laden. At least they would not get a puncture!

OCTOBER 1909. Worcestershire District Welsh Society gathering at the Baptist Chapel, Droitwich, after their Harvest Festival at St Andrews Church.

FIVE POLICEMEN who were drafted into Droitwich from an adjoining county to help local police during the 1910 election riots.

ST NICHOLAS STREET, DROITWICH. I have seen better pictures than this of a lady in her garden!

THE FUNERAL of a member of the Pond family, c. 1910.

TWO LOVELY PICTURES OF DROITWICH OPERATIC SOCIETY, containing such names as Mesdames Ethel Fisher, Connie Smith, Kath Stephens and for the men, Messrs Fabricius, Mapp, Fisher, Bourne and Baggott.

FLOWER SHOW held at Impney on 4 August 1914, the date Britain declared war on Germany.

DROITWICH FLOWER SHOW, AUGUST 1910.

TWO SUPERB PICTURES OF THE FIRE BRIGADE of Droitwich Borough and Rural District Councils.

A FINE BODY OF MEN turn out for Droitwich Early Closers 1910–1911.

THIS TIME IT IS THE TURN OF DROITWICH UNITED RESERVES, 1911–1912.

THE DROITWICH SALVATION ARMY BAND, 1919.

ST PETER'S INFANTS SCHOOL prior to the First World War.

A DELIVERY FROM THE DROITWICH STEAM BAKERY, about 1900, before the advent of plastic bread!

CELEBRATIONS IN ST GEORGE'S SQUARE for the Coronation of King George V, 22 June 1911.

THE CAMERON HIGHLANDERS at Droitwich, September 1909.

STEAM POWER, plus manpower via Mr T.A. Everton of Droitwich.

THE AFTERMATH OF A FIRE in Droitwich, 22 March 1910.

'TOGO', a dog used during the First World War, with other dogs, to collect offerings for the Red Cross.

DROITWICH SPA ORCHESTRA, Conductor Guy Magraph. 1924.

AN OLD SALT MEASURE that used to be kept in the Town Hall, Droitwich.

St Andrews Brine Baths

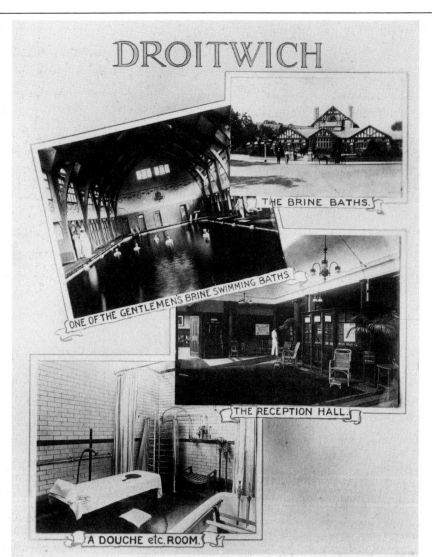

DROITWICH

THE BRINE BATHS.

ONE OF THE GENTLEMEN'S BRINE SWIMMING BATHS

THE RECEPTION HALL.

A DOUCHE etc. ROOM.

THE FAMOUS
NATURAL BRINE BATHS OF DROITWICH
Provide an effective treatment for
RHEUMATISM, NEURITIS, SCIATICA, LUMBAGO, ARTHRITIS, ETC.
Illustrated Booklet free from Joint General Managers :-

J. H. HOLLYER.
H. BERKELEY HOLLYER.   72. SPA OFFICES, DROITWICH.

THE ST ANDREW'S BRINE BATHS were another legacy from John Corbett – opened in 1882.

THE RESTFUL RECEPTION HALL at the Brine Baths.

A DISCUSSION, no doubt, on the relevant uses of brine.

THE EXTENSIONS opened by Lord Coventry, June 1907.

THE FRONT OF THE BRINE BATHS, after the extension.

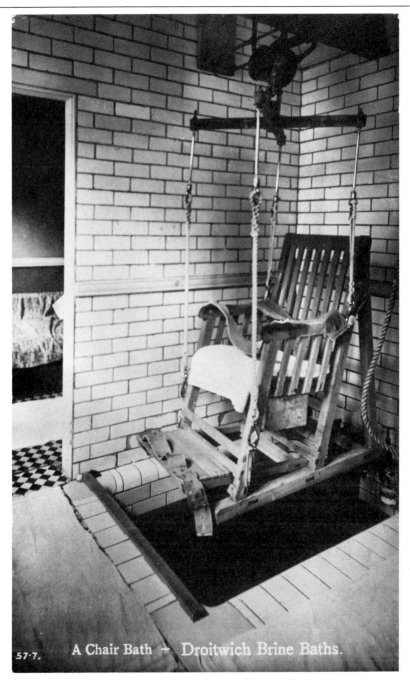

A Chair Bath – Droitwich Brine Baths.

One has not only to suffer the pain of rheumatism etc., but also to face this gruesome Chair Bath.

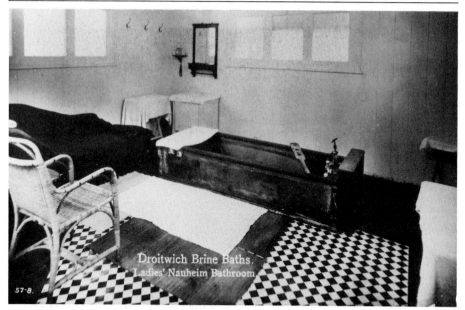

LADIES' NAUHEIM ROOM — sounds terrible!

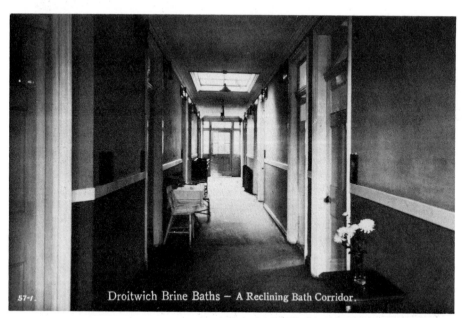

A RECLINING BATH CORRIDOR — whatever that is!

Droitwich Brine Baths
A Reclining Bath.

A RECLINING BATH. Another weird-looking piece of equipment to help the sufferers.

THE AERATION BATHS at the Brine Baths

ANOTHER AERATION BATH.

THE GENTLEMEN'S SWIMMING POOL.

Ladies' Swimming Bath, St Andrew's Brine Baths, Droitwich.

LADIES' SWIMMING POOL — no mixed bathing here!

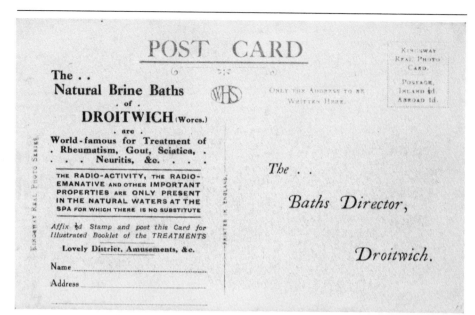

AN ADVERTISING CARD for the Brine Baths.

AN APPOINTMENT CARD, reverse side, showing you what you might get!

Places

THE WINTER GARDENS.

INSIDE THE WINTER GARDENS where tea dances, balls and conferences were held to the delight of many people.

THE LIDO. A great attraction for young and old.

THE LIDO.

THE CANAL at Wheeler's Bridge.

WHEELER'S BRIDGE from the other side.

A FURTHER VIEW OF THE CANAL.

OMBERSLEY ROAD crossing the canal bridge.

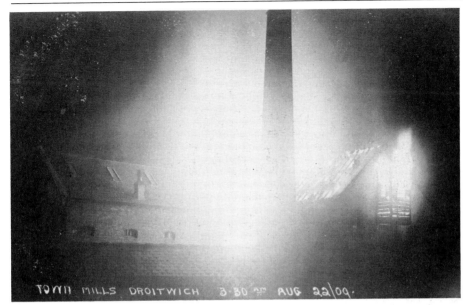

THE TOWN MILLS at the height of a fire, 3.30 a.m., 22 August 1909.

DAYLIGHT AT THE TOWN MILLS, 22 August 1909.

THE LOVELY BLACK AND WHITE COTTAGE AT HILLEND, occupied from 1890, for about 50 years, by a salt worker from Stoke Works, Mr Jack Sankey.

BROOKSIDE COTTAGES in the 1920s.

THE ROYAL BRINE BATHS built in 1836.

THE ROYAL BRINE BATHS CLINIC.

YE OLDE CURIOSITIE SHOPPE, Raven Cottage, Hillend.

NEWLAND HURST – a Home where young people with special needs are looked after with loving care and devotion.

WYCHBURY HOUSE, the home of the Curtis family for many years.

THE INTERIOR OF A CURIOSITY SHOP, August 1909, according to a message on the back of the card.

THE IMPOSING WESTWOOD PARK — the home of the Pakington family for many years.

ST PETER'S MANOR, a Tudor-style country residence, in Church Lane, Droitwich.

IN JUNE 1899, THE SPA'S NEW RAILWAY STATION WAS OPENED by Sir Frederick Godson MP, deputising for John Corbett, who was unable to attend owing to the death of a member of his family. The occasion was in the nature of a public holiday, with banners and flags festooning the approaches to the station, and hundreds of people lining the streets to view the spectacle. After the speeches, which lasted over an hour, a golden key was used to unlock the main entrance door, and the station was declared open.

THEN CAME THE PROCESSION. It was marshalled at the station approach, and, headed by the Band of the King's Shropshire Light Infantry, police and members of the Borough Council, wended its way to Salters Hall for a fine lunch and band concert. More speeches followed, mainly by important people thanking Mr Corbett for his generosity in giving much of the land on which the station was built.

Entrance, Droitwich   85680

THE ENTRANCE TO THE BRINE BATHS PARK, or is it the Lido Park or the Town Park? It has been referred to by these other names more than once. Patients from the local hospitals, clinics and hotels under the eye of John Corbett needed somewhere to relax and regain their strength, so he gave the land for a Park to be developed for the enjoyment of these and the local people.

Approach to the Park, Droitwich Spa.

WHAT YOU USED TO SEE when you entered the Park from the main road – alas, the old cannon has been melted down for 'better' things.

41640. DROITWICH, VIEW IN THE BRINE BATHS PARK.

A SECLUDED CORNER IN THE PARK.

THE TENNIS COURTS – since ripped up and fine new hard courts layed in their place in 1987.

A VIEW OF THE BOWLING GREEN.

A PEACEFUL SCENE IN THE PARK, with the bandstand, used today for Sunday concerts.

HERIOTS POOL — still popular with local fishermen.